CW00840519

Birmingham 1889

One Year in a Victorian City

Stephen Roberts

Published under the imprint *Birmingham Biographies*

Printed by CreateSpace

© Stephen Roberts, 2017

All rights reserved. No part of this publication may be reproduced in any form, stored in or re-introduced into a retrieval system, or transmitted, in any form or by any means, electronic, mechanical, photocopying, recording or otherwise without the prior consent of the author.

The moral right of Stephen Roberts to be identified as the author of this work has been asserted in accordance with the Copyright, Designs and Patents Act 1988.

ISBN-13: 978-1544139227

ISBN-10: 1544139225

Front cover: The Chamberlain fountain – known to local people as 'Squirt Square' – with the art gallery and town hall.

To the memory of Fred Roberts 1891-1946.

Contents

Acknowledgements

𝔍 have greatly enjoyed researching and writing this book. I owe thanks to a number of people. When the book was no more than an idea, Carl Chinn described it as 'a goer' and sent me useful information. My former student Joe Clinton sent me a link to a radio broadcast which provided food-for-thought. Sue Curtis generously used her skills in genealogical research on my behalf. Malcolm Dick provided helpful assistance in publicizing my work.

From the library of the Birmingham and Midland Institute I had the good fortune to be able to borrow for an extended period the two relevant volumes of the Birmingham satirical magazines the *Dart* and the *Owl.* The cartoons included here are reproduced by permission of the BMI. The resources of the Library of Birmingham have been invaluable and the staff, as ever, very helpful. I have also benefitted from consulting provincial newspapers provided by the British Newspaper Archive.

This book is dedicated to the memory of my grandfather Fred Roberts ... not a Brum by birth but a Brum all the same.

Author's Note

In 1889 the people of Birmingham described themselves as 'Brums' rather than as 'Brummies' – a practice I have followed here.

Preface

On 1 November 1838, the charter of incorporation was received in Birmingham. Within two months the thirteen newly-created wards had elected a town council, made up entirely of supporters of this new move. The charter mayor was William Scholefield, up to this point high bailiff. The powers of the new council were restricted, with the self-appointed street commissioners still playing an important part in the governance of the town. Nevertheless, this was a great triumph for Birmingham reformers after prolonged and fierce opposition from vested interests, and was celebrated with a public dinner at the town hall on 21 February 1839. With 'a numerous assemblage of well-attired females in the galleries' looking on, five hundred gentlemen sat down to a dinner – 'including desert and a pint of wine' – which, with songs and toasts, lasted for six hours.[1] The charter, the town clerk William Redfern, declared was 'a precious deposit ... the foundation of our local rights and liberties ... our Magna Carta.'[2] In 1851 those local rights were extended with the abolition of the street commissioners and the town council became solely responsible for the governance of this growing industrial town.

'It is most curious', the *Birmingham Daily Post* remarked in autumn 1888, 'that the jubilee year of the Birmingham corporation should have been allowed to run its course so far apparently unnoticed or at any rate without eliciting a single proposal for its due commemoration.'[3] The mayor reported that the issue had not been raised with him, though 'the matter ... was never absent from his mind.'[4] The men who led the campaign for incorporation and might have said something were mostly all dead – George Muntz in 1857, William Scholefield in 1867 and George Edmonds in 1868.[5]

---

[1] *Aris's Birmingham Gazette,* 25 February 1839; *Birmingham Journal,* 21 February 1839. C. Gill, *History of Birmingham* (Oxford, 1952), pp. 219-39.
[2] *Birmingham Journal,* 23 February 1839.
[3] *Birmingham Daily Post,* 12 October 1889.
[4] Ibid., 24 October 1888.
[5] See obits., *Birmingham Journal,* 1 August 1857; *Birmingham Daily Post,* 10 July 1867, 4 July 1868.

Fortuitously one of them, perhaps the most important of all, was still alive. Philip Henry Muntz, younger brother of George Muntz, was seventy-seven years old, and had been the instigator of the public meeting in January 1837 that launched the campaign for incorporation. Succeeding Scholefield as mayor in 1839, he had later gone on represent Birmingham in Parliament. Seemingly at the suggestion of the editor of the *Post* J.T. Bunce, arrangements were speedily made to offer Muntz the freedom of the town to mark the anniversary. Muntz made clear to friends that he 'was very eager for the liberty of the town that he loved so well'; and so on 31 October 1888 a special meeting of the town council was convened to present Muntz with the freedom of the town.[6] In his speech Muntz recalled the 'ordeal' of securing the charter in the face of 'apathy ... which was to him incomprehensible' and 'an opposition, the virulence of which was extraordinary'.[7]

Honouring one man, however, did not seem enough. Another five-hour long dinner for leading gentlemen in the town hall, with their wives and daughters as spectators in the galleries, was clearly out of the question. It was at this point that the town clerk Edward Orford Smith had his bright idea. With eighteen years' experience as a solicitor, Smith had been appointed town clerk in August 1881. 'I am ... the principal permanent official of the corporation, the chief of staff, so to speak', Smith opined. 'As such I must know a good deal and I hope I think a good deal ...'[8] His thinking on the matter of the jubilee led to a proposal that Birmingham should seek city status. Belfast had recently acquired city status, and Manchester (1853) Liverpool (1880) and Newcastle (1882) had become cities when bishops had been appointed. Birmingham's claim seemed unassailable: 'So important was the work of the council that the council became a training ground for Parliament ... The municipal work done here during the last fifty years can hardly have been surpassed.'[9] With the approval of the mayor, Smith wrote to the Home Office. At this point the town council was kept in the dark, and the plan did not become known across the town until it was announced in the *Birmingham Daily Post* at the end of November.

---

[6] Ibid., 24 October 1888.
[7] Ibid., 1 November 1888.
[8] *Birmingham Faces and Places,* I (1889), pp. 147-8.
[9] *Birmingham Daily Post,* 1 November, 30 November 1888.

Early in December a petition was adopted by the town council and sent to the Home Secretary Henry Matthews asking the Queen to approve the elevation of Birmingham to city status. It cannot be said that the proposal provoked great excitement amongst the councillors. 'Out of town' one observed, 'there were some people who might pay more respect to Birmingham if it were a city and at any rate it would do no harm'; and another wondered whether 'the mace would be introduced and tinsel baubles would become familiar to them and whether they would be required to wear robes. He hoped, however, that Birmingham ... would prefer doing good public work to bedizening itself with any of these things.'[10]

So it was Edward Orford Smith who secured city status for Birmingham. His obituarist described him as 'one of the men who must be reckoned amongst the most important in any list of the makers of modern Birmingham ... for many years his opinion was one of the chief influences in directing the council in its decisions.'[11] Yet this man is now entirely forgotten. Born in Romney in Kent on 21 November 1841, Smith was the son of a clergyman. His mother was French, with connections to Napoleon: one of his most prized possessions was a small marble statue of the French emperor. Fluent in French, Smith also professed a liking for French cuisine. He was educated at Marlborough College in Wiltshire and in Dresden, where he acquired a proficiency in German.

The town clerk offered legal advice to the council and the position was filled by a solicitor. Smith, aged forty at the time of his appointment, had worked at the highest levels of his profession. Articled to a Maidstone solicitor who was a friend of his father's in 1858, he had progressed to work as a solicitor in London, where he managed the parliamentary business of railway companies, and in Solihull, where he was clerk to the sanitary authority and the Board of Guardians. He was one of thirty-four applicants for the post of town clerk in Birmingham when it was advertised on a salary of £2000 a year, an increase of £800 on the salary of the retiring clerk. An attempt was made by town councillors to reduce his salary after his selection. 'However good Mr Smith might be', one councillor observed, 'he did not consider him a £2000 man.'[12] Smith,

---

[10] Ibid., 5 December 1888.
[11] *Birmingham Daily Mail,* 30 December 1915.
[12] *Birmingham Daily Post,* 24 August 1881.

however, made clear that he would only accept the post on its advertised terms. In his work Smith was assisted by an office of clerks and solicitors, eventually amounting to about a dozen. In 1883 he oversaw the Birmingham (Consolidation) Act, which brought together a range of legislation relating to the governance of the town. In 1892 he instigated the Birmingham Corporation Water Act, which enabled the compulsory purchase of the Elan valley.[13] It was said that Smith's advice ensured that all legal actions against the council relating to the Improvement Scheme were defeated.[14]

Smith did not live in Birmingham, but twenty miles away at The Lodge in Leek Wootton, Warwickshire. His wife was called Mary, as was his only surviving child.[15] Away from his occupation, he took a great interest in cricket. As a result of ill health, Smith retired as town clerk in 1907. Shortly afterwards the family moved to Leamington Spa, where Smith employed an invalid assistant. He died on 29 December 1915.[16]

Described at the time of his appointment as 'a gentleman of a pleasing manner', Smith had a forceful manner and could also be cold and aloof.[17] 'He was perhaps something of an autocrat in his own sphere', it was recalled, 'with some of the expert's contempt for the ill-informed opinions of the layman; more than one councillor who ventured to differ from him on a point of policy found himself sharply, and even sarcastically answered, before other members of the council.'[18] Unlike many men in late Victorian Birmingham, who

---

[13] This new supply of water for Birmingham came into operation in 1904. Little or no compensation was paid to those farming in the area before it was acquired by the city council.

[14] Under the Improvement Scheme, the development of an extensive area of freehold land acquired by the council in 1876 was undertaken. Corporation Street was the central feature.

[15] His daughter Mary was born in 1873. A son was still born in 1867 and a daughter died aged three weeks in 1871: *Birmingham Daily Post,* 27 February 1867, 16 September, 6 October 1871.

[16] Smith's estate amounted to £5,893 11s. 9d. He left £100 to a servant who had been with him for many years, and one year's wages to his two other servants. His wife was the main beneficiary of his will, with his daughter receiving £200.

[17] *Birmingham Daily Post,* 24 August 1884.

[18] *Birmingham Daily Mail,* 30 December 1915.

demonstrated their 'manliness' by sporting untrimmed beards, neck beards and Piccadilly weepers, Smith remained resolutely clean-shaven.

January

With Birmingham afflicted by freezing fog and the skaters out in strength on the pool in Aston Park, some of more well-heeled residents began to consider retreating for a few weeks to their favourite summer destinations, the resorts of North Wales. Hotels took out advertisements in the Birmingham periodicals, offering a winter 'pick-me-up' for two guineas a week.[1] One correspondent to the *Dart* certainly felt rejuvenated after the fortnight he spent at the Marine Hotel in Barmouth, where 'sheltered ... from north and east winds by the picturesque mountains at the back and receiving the soft breezes of the south and west ... the weather ... (was) warm and genial as in the middle of summer'.[2]

For those unable to escape 'this murky, dissipated town – ahem! city - of ours' with a break by the seaside, there was another, immensely popular, form of escape – the pantomime.[3] For 'Dick Whittington' at the Theatre Royal in New Street 'nightly hundreds are turned away, not being able to gain admittance ...' and there were also large audiences for the afternoon and evening performances of 'Bluebeard' at the Prince of Wales Theatre in Broad Street and 'Bo-Peep' at the Grand Theatre in Corporation Street.[4] The leading parts in these productions were played by performers who were well-known in music halls across the country. Vesta Tilley was able to command £50 a week during her appearances in Birmingham as the principal boy in 'Dick Whittington', her songs being 'on everybody's lips'.[5] The rising star Alice Leamar appeared as 'Bo-Peep' 'a part which she fills as an ideal which will long live in the memories of Birmingham play

---

[1] The *Dart*, 4 January 1889.
[2] Ibid., 1 February 1889.
[3] The *Owl*, 4 January 1889.
[4] The *Dart*, 28 January 1889. The Queen's Theatre in Snow Hill was putting on plays this month.
[5] The *Dart*, 4 January 1889. Vesta Tilley was the stage name of Matilda Alice Powles (1864-1952), who achieved great celebrity as a male impersonator; as well as playing 'Dick Whittington' in pantomimes, she created comic portrayals of fops, clergymen and soldiers.

goers'.[6] The *Owl*, each week full of opinion about the various productions, began printing coupons to enable readers to nominate the best performer of the season – the winner was promised a large cake. It claimed that 'the coupons are coming rolling in and we are beginning to fear we shall have to hire a couple of extra clerks to count the votes each week.'[7] At the head of the poll at the end of the month was the Glasgow-born entertainer Marie Loftus, who was appearing in 'Bluebeard' at the Prince of Wales Theatre.

The female stars of the pantomime however, had more than just the cake on their minds. At the end of performances they found themselves being followed by small groups of young men and, as they descended from their carriages, being asked for money. Marie Loftus refused to pay up, and as a result was hissed and booed during subsequent appearances. 'They made it warm for me the next Saturday night', she observed during a long interview with a local newspaper. 'They made such a row in the gallery that my songs were spoiled and I could not make a word travel anyhow ... Birmingham is the worst place in England for blackmail.'[8] It became necessary for Marie Loftus to ask for a police constable to be present at her lodgings when she returned from the theatre, and arrests were made.

It wasn't only the pantomime stars who aired their complaints in the newspapers. There were, one correspondent reported, groups of working class men who 'perambulate our streets and make night hideous with their frightful yells of stupid rhymes.'[9] Another was dissatisfied with street lighting when there was fog: 'This morning it was so dense in the middle of town that it was impossible to see two yards before one ... we were left to grope our way across the streets where several roads meet as best we could.'[10] Yet another letter-writer was vexed by the standard of dress of the guards on the trams, who did not wear uniforms but sported 'coats tied together with string and shirts about the colour of a soot bag';

---

[6] Ibid., 11 January 1889. Alice Leamar (b. 1870) began to regularly appear at London music halls in 1883 and the following year made her debut in pantomime in Portsmouth.

[7] The *Owl*, 25 January 1889.

[8] *Birmingham Evening Mail*, 28 January 1889.

[9] *Birmingham Daily Post*, 2 January 1889.

[10] Ibid., 4 January 1889.

one guard replied, stating that he only earned eighteen shillings a week and had been fined 2s. 6d. on several occasions 'for very trifling matters such as nipping a ticket in the wrong section.'[11]

This was the month of annual balls and concerts. The most prestigious venues for these occasions were the town hall or the assembly rooms in Edgbaston. And so members of the Primrose League, volunteer soldiers, amateur swimmers, grocers, chemists and others danced until the early hours on these winter nights, warming themselves with a cup of beef tea before stepping outside. All this dancing stirred the newspaper correspondents into action. 'An Anxious Bachelor', concerned that young women were not spending enough time reading and honing their domestic skills, expressed his view that three dances a week really was too much; 'Ethel' informed him that dancing was 'a healthful and harmless amusement ... (which) helps to cheer the evenings at the end of a hard day's work in this depressing weather.'[12]

'Birmingham is more agreeable than it was even a dozen years ago', the *Dart* observed at the beginning of the year. 'There are now noble streets and buildings to admire, many business places are in themselves attractive and our reading rooms and art galleries are visited and admired.'[13] The newly-laid out Corporation Street was 'both in an architectural and a sanitary aspect ... advantageous and ornamental to the city.'[14] After inspecting the new shops, visitors and locals had a growing range of restaurants to choose from. The Hen and Chickens in New Street prided itself on being the most esteemed hotel in Birmingham, and in its famous grill leading local figures were able to eat their dinners using silver cutlery. The Acorn Hotel in Temple Street claimed that it had 'the finest grill room in Birmingham ... (and) free lavatories' whilst the Windsor restaurant in Cannon Street boasted that they had managed to lure away from the Hen and Chickens 'the well-known chef William' to prepare their hot joints, chops and steaks.[15] For fish, Pope's

---

[11] Ibid., 12 January, 14 January, 17 January, 18 January 1889. Apparently, the fines funded sick pay.
[12] Ibid., 12 January, 14 January, 15 January, 16 January, 17 January 1889.
[13] The *Dart,* 4 January 1889.
[14] Ibid., 18 January 1889.
[15] Ibid., 4 January 1889; the *Owl,* 4 January 1889.

3

restaurant, also in Cannon Street, was highly regarded – boiled turbot and lobster sauce, fried eels and devilled sardines on toast were its specialities. For those who wanted to pretend they were dining in Paris or Berlin, there was the Continental Restaurant in New Street, offering conversation in French or German alongside five courses for 1s. 9d. There were also nine clubs in Birmingham which provided dining for their members, including the Liberal Club, the Conservative Club and, for those who wished to discuss association football and racing over their suppers, the Birmingham Club.

The first season of the Football League was drawing to a close, and Aston Villa were on their way to finishing as runners-up, well behind Preston North End. Home matches were played at Wellington Road in Perry Barr, attracting crowds of up to 10,000. Here, earlier in the season, Notts County and Blackburn Rovers had been despatched 9-1 and 6-1 respectively. However, in the first match of 1889 at Burnley, the team lost 4-0. For the *Burnley Gazette* it was a 'crushing defeat', Burnley being 'in grand form all round', but the *Owl* saw it very differently: 'Archie Hunter was absent from the team while Freddy Dawson, who was picked to play, failed to turn up at the railway station. Consequently, the Brums had ten men on the field at Turf Moor, which considerably discounts Burnley's performance.'[16] That weekend Wolverhampton Wanderers triumphed 3-1 over WBA, an undeserved defeat according to the *Owl*, which bemoaned the 'vile luck' of 'the most unfortunate eleven playing on the English football field'.[17] Meanwhile, in the Football Alliance, 'the Small Heath boys had a day out against Notts Olympic and, going by the score, must have enjoyed themselves immensely.'[18]

Birmingham returned seven MPs to the House of Commons. Seventy-eight year old John Bright was the longest-serving, having first been elected in 1858. Joseph Chamberlain joined him in 1876.

---

[16] *Burnley Gazette,* 9 January 1889; the *Owl,* 11 January 1889. Archie Hunter (1859-94) was the Villa's celebrated captain; he retired after suffering a heart attack during a match in 1890. Freddie Dawson played only three matches for the Villa in the 1888-9 season.

[17] The *Owl,* 18 January 1889.

[18] Ibid. The Football Alliance became the second tier of the Football League in 1892.

4

This was a turbulent time in politics, and the turbulence was felt no more strongly than in Birmingham. Chamberlain's break with Gladstone over Irish Home Rule in 1886 saw the once all-powerful Birmingham Liberal Association reduced to a supporting role in local politics. The Liberal Unionists, in uneasy alliance with the Tories, were the dominant political force. Joe's right-hand men Jesse Collings and Joseph Powell Williams joined him in the Commons, and J.T. Bunce steered a firmly pro-Chamberlain in the *Birmingham Daily Post.* The only real voices of dissent were the satirical magazines. The *Dart* had been critical of Joe since its inception in 1876, accusing him of self-glorification and convening a governing clique. When, in January, it announced that the Revd. S. Williams, a leading Nonconformist minister, was leaving Birmingham, it attributed this to political suffocation, the city 'not what it has been ... for men of large minds, high education and broad views.'[19] The *Owl,* a Liberal publication provided with funds by the Cornish-born businessman Richard Tangye, turned against Chamberlain with great venom after the Home Rule split. However, in January the magazine had yet to get into its full vitriolic stride and began the year by gently poking fun at twenty-five year old Austen Chamberlain, whose father had recently married for a third time, his wife being Mary Endicott. This development, the *Owl* imagined, left his eldest son Austen in a quandary:

> I'm in a fix, I must admit;
> In fact I'm quite embarrassed;
> How my new ma I should address
> Has made me warm and vexed.
> She is very young, you know,
> I cannot say "dear mother",
> Such a title seems to me absurd,
> Yet I can find no other.
> To call her "Mrs Chamberlain" is clearly infra dig,
> And "Mary's" rather intimate,
> And pa thinks I'm too big;
> I really can't tell what to do,
> It haunts me like a ghost;
> Ah! happy thought, I'll write at once,

---

[19] The *Dart,* 11 January 1889.

And ask the *Daily Post*.[20]

The town council, made up of forty-eight councillors and sixteen aldermen, met once a month. When these gentlemen gathered for the first time in 1889, they discovered that the charter raising the town to the status of city had not yet been received. 'As no one seemed to care a straw about the matter', it was reported, 'there was no disappointment expressed and the matter was quickly passed over.'[21]

---

[20] The *Owl*, 11 January 1889. Joseph Chamberlain and his wife returned from their honeymoon in January 1889; Mary Chamberlain was presented with a pearl necklace, a star of diamonds and gold bracelets on behalf of the people of Birmingham at the town hall and these were displayed in the art gallery.
[21] The *Dart*, 11 January 1889; *Birmingham Daily Post*, 9 January 1889. The only observation made was that by a councillor who wanted to know if the new city status would result in an increase in the rates which 'were already heavy enough.'

February

*A*t the first meeting of the newly-created city council, the charter was read by the mayor Richard Cadbury Barrow and the general purposes committee was charged with commissioning a new city coat of arms. That apart, it was business as normal: the councillors settled down for a discussion about electric lighting in the streets and agreed that this should be left to private enterprise. 'There was no special display to mark the occasion', it was reported, 'and to the disappointment of many even the town clerk did not don gown and wig to give lustre to the "city" dignity which he had been so instrumental in procuring.'[1] Absent from the meeting were 'Mr Middlemore, who has practically abandoned council work, and Messrs. Clayton and Wallis, who, when last heard of, were wandering in the Egyptian desert and were bound for Jericho'.[2] Intending to get on the council was Austen Chamberlain. When it became known that he would be contesting St. Thomas' ward in November, the *Owl* was dismissive and hostile: he was 'the snobbish boy' and 'the sole motive of the Unionist tactics is selfishness and place hunting for the Chamberlain family.'[3]

The Birmingham Liberal Association meanwhile sought to prevent Joe from having it all his own way with a large meeting in the town hall. The rallying cry was the treatment of incarcerated Irish agitators. 'That fine old radical performer ...', the Baptist minister Arthur O'Neill, the barrister and political man-on-the-rise Herbert Asquith and the parliamentary champion of Fenian prisoners John O'Connor Power all expressed their dismay that 'in order to prop up a rotten system of landlordism ... Irish patriots

---

[1] The *Dart,* 8 February 1889; *Birmingham Daily Post,* 2 February, 6 February 1889.
[2] The *Dart,* 1 February 1889. John Throgmorton Middlemore was a member of a prominent Birmingham family and councillor for Nechells, serving on the health committee. He devoted much time to the organisation of emigration schemes for poor children to Canada. Charles Wallis was a councillor for Edgbaston. Francis Clayton was a councillor for Rotton Park and highly-regarded chairman of the finance committee. He served as mayor in 1889-90.
[3] The *Owl,* 15 February, 22 February 1889.

should be degraded and mistreated.'[4] Another cause that got an airing at a meeting in the town hall was that of protection. According to reports, H.J. Pettifer, a one-time Birmingham electroplater and now secretary of the Working Men's Association for the Defence of British Industries, had, according to preference, been 'sensible and convincing' or had 'finally sunk in the Fair Trade bog.'[5]

The pantomimes continued to attract large audiences, with 'Bo-Peep' having 'to turn money away from every performance ...'[6] That some were admitted when there were no seats and people standing did caused disgruntlement, one dissatisfied theatre-goer complaining that 'a large amount of money must have been taken from people who have not seen the performances at all ...'[7] The cake competition organised by the *Owl* was still running. One voter submitted his vote for the prettiest performer and was duly ticked off: 'This is quite wrong ... Beauty competitions are acceptable only to Pears' Soap Company. The *Owl*'s Genoa will be won, and given to, genuine merit.'[8] It was rumoured that Marie Loftus did not want to win a cake but her withdrawal from the contest was ruled to be not possible 'unless she first obtains the consent of her admirers.'[9] At the end of the month she duly won a three-tier cake, having secured 1,891 votes. She was also presented with a stand of flowers which was four feet tall and other bouquets, all of which were sent to the Queen's Hospital. Vesta Tilley and Alice Leamar were second and third in the contest with 1,538 and 1,119 votes respectively. 'Pretty as a picture, light as a snow flake and modest as a daisy ...' the *Owl* sighed as Alice bid farewell to Birmingham.[10] Dick Whittington's horse tied for last place with a cat and Bo-Peep's sheep, each securing one vote each.

A shilling – or four shillings for reserved seats – bought entry to the Masonic Hall in New Street for a piano recital by Max Pauer;

---

[4] The *Owl*, 15 February 1889; *Birmingham Daily Post*, 12 February 1889.
[5] The *Dart*, 1 February 1889; the *Owl*, 8 February 1889; *Birmingham Daily Post*, 6 February 1889.
[6] The *Owl*, 1 February 1889.
[7] *Birmingham Daily Post*, 26 February 1889.
[8] The *Owl*, 8 February 1889.
[9] Ibid.
[10] Ibid. 1 February 1889.

though the son of a famous pianist, the event was not well-attended. For the same prices, the 'wonderful boy pianist' Otto Hegner attracted greater numbers to the town hall the following week.[11] At Day's Concert Hall 'Miss Patty Heywood ... ha(d) some splendid frocks, some ugly hats and new songs' whilst at Bristol Street Board School an 'exceedingly funny' production was put on to raise funds to buy shoes for poor children and featured the London actress Ethel Davis, who 'creat(ed) quite a furore, encore after encore being demanded.'[12] At the workhouse in Gravelly Hill a concert for the inmates by the Erdington Harmonic Society 'passed off with great elat'.[13]

In his quest to make Corporation Street a prestigious shopping area, Joseph Chamberlain strove to secure the opening of a Lewis' department store. At a cost of £30,000 the new seven storey store – with views of up to twenty miles from its roof - opened in September 1885, with a large selection of clothing for men, women and children.[14] This month an entire floor of the store was given over to promoting Japan and Japanese goods. There were Japanese assistants, dressed in kimonos and engaged in bamboo-cutting, fan-making and the like, and, each afternoon, entertainment Japanese-style. Admission cost one penny, with a present given in return. It was hugely popular, with 24,000 visitors in the first three weeks. Another event which attracted the crowds was a photographic exhibition, including a ladies category, in the art gallery.

'Tremendous interest is centred on the meeting of North End and Aston Villa', a Lancashire newspaper reported, 'as the clubs are respectively first and second in the League championship, while the Preston club have never suffered defeat in a League encounter.'[15] At Perry Barr in 'a magnificent game' watched by a crowd of 12,000 wrapped up against the bitter cold, Preston North End held on to their unbeaten record, winning 2-0. Villa did, however, make progress in the F.A. Cup, defeating Derby County, who had sought to have the fixture abandoned due to the Perry Barr pitch being 'in

---

[11] Ibid., 8 February 1889.
[12] Ibid.; ibid., 22 February 1889.
[13] The *Dart,* 15 February 1889.
[14] See *Birmingham Daily Post,* 18 September 1885.
[15] *Preston Herald,* 9 February 1889.

a wretched state, one end of the field being a perfect quagmire.'[16] West Bromwich Albion and Wolverhampton Wanderers won their fixtures this month, both racking up goals in the F.A. Cup.

Fanny Locker, 'a weird-looking old woman', found herself imprisoned for two months for telling fortunes for money. [17] The police had turned a blind eye to her activities until business picked up. Two women had visited her and she had 'demanded money and then said they would each inherit fabulous wealth'; another patron of her services was left 'mentally deranged' after being informed that her husband was paying attention to another woman.[18] Also in trouble was William Bailsford, who, on his arrival in Birmingham, claimed to be a retired a single man and took a bar maid as his wife; when it was discovered that he had left behind a wife in Gloucester, he was sentenced to six months for bigamy.

In the letters columns of the newspapers Brums were letting off steam. Rain flowing from roofs onto foot paths was 'nothing less than abominable' and the steam trams were 'an abominable nuisance ... The noise they make ... is enough to frighten anyone, let alone horses.'[19] And then there was the town hall which was very uncomfortable a result of 'the obnoxious atmosphere ... the place ... (is) as hot as the tropical plant house at the botanical gardens.'[20] The satirical magazines were disgruntled by what they observed in the streets – horses pulling omnibuses that ought to be retired and employees of undertakers visiting public houses during internments as Warstone Lane, 'a scandalous and disgusting sight'.[21] But at least the stipendiary magistrate had re-introduced birching, 'the most harmless and at the same time effectual means of putting a check on juvenile depravity ...'[22] And Pope's restaurant was still 'the one place in town for a really enjoyable fish snack' and there were

---

[16] *Derby Daily Telegraph*, 18 February 1889.
[17] *Western Daily Press*, 26 February 1889.
[18] *Worcester Journal*, 26 February 1889.
[19] *Birmingham Daily Post*, 3 February, 9 February 1889.
[20] Ibid., 26 February 1889.
[21] The *Dart*, 15 February 1889.
[22] Ibid., 22 February 1889.

excellent Valentine's cards to be obtained from Blackett's in New Street.[23]

In the middle of the month heavy snow fell across the city and 'rendered traffic extremely difficult ... travelling by tram and bus has been greatly impeded'; but a thaw quickly set in.[24]

---

[23] Ibid., 1 February 1889.
[24] *Northampton Mercury,* 16 February 1889.

March

The opening of Hengler's Grand Cirque at Curzon Hall in Suffolk Street at the beginning of the month aroused great excitement across the city. The son of a tightrope artist and himself an equestrian, Charles Hengler - and, after his death, his son Albert - managed the most celebrated circus in Victorian Britain.[1] For three hours each evening, Brums were able to enjoy clowns, impressionists, jugglers, acrobats, equestrians and performing animals. With the content varied with each performance, people went again and again. It was reported that many thousands attended the circus during its stay. The satirical magazines were thrilled by it all: the clowns Whimsical Walker and Funny Fred Hall were 'excruciatingly funny', the acrobats Sibb and Sibb 'marvellous' and the elephants, Waddy, Molly and Boney, were, in walking on their hind legs or riding a tricycle, 'quite too awfully funny.'[2] If all of this wasn't enough, Marie Loftus was back at the Gaiety, the town's leading music hall, and the 'sensational' ventriloquist and magician Hercat was also 'nightly delighting crowded audiences' at Day's Crystal Palace Concert Hall.[3] He was accompanied by Fay Rivington, 'a bewitchingly pretty young lady.'[4]

It was reported that, as he performed his tricks, Boney, the youngest of the elephants at the circus, 'squeals and grunts in youthful glee ...'[5] The correspondents to the newspapers, however, were sure that the horses that pulled the omnibuses were strangers

[1] Charles Hengler (1821-87) was a shrewd businessman: he recognised that commercial success lay in employing the most talented performers and ensuring that all shows ran smoothly. See John M. Turner, 'Hengler's Circus and Gloucestershire', *Gloucestershire History* (1989), no. 3, pp. 4-5.
[2] The *Owl*, 22 February 1889; the *Dart*, 8, 15 1889.
[3] Situated on the corner of Smallbrook Street and Hurst Street and owned by James Day, the concert hall was lavishly decorated. Built in 1862, it closed in 1893 and was demolished.
[4] The *Dart*, 8 March 1889; the *Owl*, 15 March 1889. Hercat was the stage name of R.D. Chater (1836-1913). To add to his allure, he allowed audiences to think that he was American but he had in fact only visited the country and had been born in Britain.
[5] *Birmingham Daily Post*, 4 March 1889.

to glee. They reported the 'inhuman exhibitions' they witnessed in the streets, including whipping 'every two yards'; it is 'truly pitiable to see the poor creatures and it is a disgrace to the community', one correspondent wrote.[6] A Steam Tram Anti-Nuisance Association was also formed, and its secretary wrote in to complain that these vehicles, which carried sixty passengers, frightened horses and damaged property.

For Aston Villa it was a calamitous month. An 8-1 defeat away at Blackburn Rovers in the F.A. Cup was followed by a 5-2 defeat away at Derby County in the Football League, when the team, reduced to ten men in the second half, 'never had a look in ... (and) played a straggling game, appearing to be quite disorganised.'[7] 'Spoiled by success and flattery', the *Dart* observed, the players have gone to pieces'; 'the popularity of the Villa has greatly lessened', it continued, complaining that 'a want a continuous recruiting is the defect' and 'public housekeeping is not the best occupation for athletes to follow'.[8] West Bromwich Albion, meanwhile, were defeated 1-0 in the semi-final of the F.A. Cup by the all-conquering Preston North End, who then despatched Wolverhampton Wanderers 3-0 in the final. To see what baseball was all about, a game featuring American players was staged in Edgbaston, but it 'did not create a very great impression upon the minds of Birmingham people who seemed to think it was a skilful exhibition but an awfully slow and tame game ...'[9]

Meanwhile, at the Birmingham and Midland Institute, there was a dramatic turn-of-events. The secretary Paxton Porter was arrested on a charge of embezzlement. He had held the post for a decade 'at a large salary and was a considerable figure in Birmingham society'.[10] The *Dart,* however, had long had its suspicions about him: 'He did not come to business till twelve o'clock and was off at one to lunch and games of chess lasting far into the afternoon.'[11] Pleading guilty to embezzling £1,200, Paxton Porter was sentenced to five years in prison; he was released in

---

[6] Ibid., 12 March, 21 March 1889.
[7] *Derby Daily Telegraph,* 11 March 1889.
[8] The *Dart,* 15 March, 5 April 1889.
[9] *Hull Daily Mail,* 18 March 1889.
[10] *Huddersfield Chronicle,* 2 March 1889.
[11] The *Dart,* 8 March 1889.

December 1892.[12] Also locked up this month was A.J. Roadway, the curator of Aston Hall; he was convicted of defrauding the baths and parks committee of the city council.

The *Dart* continued its long campaign against Chamberlain and his circle, poking fun at the political ambitions of 'Master Austen' and seeing in the city council's usurpation of the sale of gas fitting from private contractors 'a glaring injustice, born of the Chamberlain reign ... The Corporation has no more business to deal in gas fittings than it has to sell pork pies or boots or shoes.'[13]

On 27 March John Bright died. Defeated in Manchester over his opposition to the Crimean War, he had been brought forward in Birmingham thirty-one years earlier to cement the town's reform credentials. Over this long period, Bright in fact had very little to do with the town that sent him to the House of Commons. He appeared once or twice a year for a few days to make a well-reported speech in the town hall, staying with either Chamberlain or Dixon. His election expenses were paid for him, and he did not contribute to charitable causes in the town. With his death the local Tories expected to field their candidate of 1885 Lord Randolph Churchill in the by-election in Central Birmingham, believing that Chamberlain had indicated his support for this arrangement to their chairman Sir James – Sir Jeems, according to the *Dart* –Sawyer during a dinner at Highbury.[14] The much-weakened BLA, meanwhile, equivocated over whether to bring forward a candidate: 'With the purse, organisation and press of the Family against him, success would be miraculous ... the party must not be disgraced by a hopeless candidature and an ignominious defeat.'[15]

---

[12] *Birmingham Daily Post,* 8 March, 12 March 1889, 29 December 1892 for full details.
[13] The *Dart*, 15 March, 22 March 1889.
[14] Ibid., 1 March 1889.
[15] The *Owl*, 29 March 1889.

April

Whatever Chamberlain might have said to local Tory leaders – and he denied any compact had been made – neither Lord Randolph Churchill nor any other Tory came forward in the by-election in Central Birmingham.[1] Moving quickly, Chamberlain ensured that the candidate was Bright's son, Albert. Jesse Collings, MP for Bordesley and Chamberlain's 'faithful political valet', declared, 'We hold the Tories in the hollow of our hand ... and he who denies this, knows nothing about it.'[2] The Tory solicitor Joseph Rowlands believed that his party had been 'sold'. Resigning as chairman of his local party, he was candid in his comments: 'Mr Bright is brought forward in breach of good faith and I, for one, decline to support him'.[3] The damage to the Liberal Unionist-Conservative alliance in Birmingham was considerable. In these circumstances, the BLA concluded that this might well be their moment and brought forward the barrister William Phipson Beale to contest the seat. He addressed meetings in favour of Home Rule but most effort was put into exploiting the fissure in the Unionist alliance: 'CONSERVATIVES! DON'T BE HUMBUGGED! ... Keep away from the polls or, if you must vote, VOTE FOR BEALE and teach Mr Chamberlain a lesson he richly deserves. Mr Beale's return will not be a Home Rule victory but a Conservative triumph ...'[4]

Though he accepted the offer to stand in Central Birmingham, John Albert Bright was not at all keen on meeting the voters. Prevailed upon to do something, he paid a couple of brief visits to the constituency. The *Owl* was distinctly unimpressed by his speeches, referring to 'his schoolboy sentences ... a dozen spoken words and a full stop. Poor John Albert! What a fool to follow his father. Impudence succeeding Dignity is the picture!'[5] The *Dart* joined in, referring to 'that ninny John Albert ... As my father was,

---

[1] R. Rhodes James, *Lord Randolph Churchill* (1986 edn.), pp. 333-6.
[2] *Western Daily News,* 25 April 1889.
[3] *Birmingham Daily Gazette,* 9 April 1889.
[4] The *Owl,* 12 April 1889.
[5] Ibid.

so I will be, baring the ability.'[6] The Liberal Unionist candidate was promoted by the pro-Chamberlain local press as 'Mr Bright' and Tory voters, urged on by a visiting minister Arthur Balfour and with Chamberlain nowhere to be seen, came out to support him:

Bright: 5621
Beale: 2561
Majority: 3060

It was, the *Owl* admitted, 'an awful thrashing ... In the ... Liberal Club the result was received with sad amusement ... one lady cried outright and Mr Beale looked as it would have been a relief to do the same.'[7]

Amidst the political tumult, life went on. Hengler's circus entered its last few weeks and Felix Mendelssohn's 'Elijah' was performed at the town hall. Easter visits to Llandudno and Bournemouth were undertaken, and excursions arranged to see the Atlantic liners at Liverpool. Three thousand poor children enjoyed coffee – over four hundred gallons was provided - buns and religious music at Bingley Hall; they had to bring their own cups or tins but everything else was provided by the Tory merchant and philanthropist Amos Roe.

---

[6] The *Dart,* 5 April, 12 April 1889.
[7] *The Owl*, 19 April 1889.

May

The repercussions of the by-election in Central Birmingham were to be long felt. Sir James Sawyer became the second casualty in the Tory camp. 'I find myself unable to draw a distinction between myself and Mr Rowlands', he wrote in his letter resigning as president of the Birmingham Conservative Association. 'I could not again trust the leaders of the Liberal Unionist party in Birmingham'.[1] The *Dart* believed that the Tories had no one to blame but themselves for the way they had been treated by Chamberlain: 'As soon as the charmer chooses to pipe, they commence to dance, lose their heads and become his tools'.[2] And so the Tories were left with just one MP – the Home Secretary Henry Matthews in East Birmingham, depicted in the satirical magazines as 'the wobbling creature' and 'Mr Muddle Matthews'.[3] For the Liberals, humiliated in the by-election, there was nothing that could be done but to launch bitter attack after bitter attack on Joe and Albert Bright. The latter was declared to be 'a coward ... he ... need not show his face in the constituency again. So button up your pockets, Johnny; be as miserly as your father and election times will always find some greenhorns ready to pay your expenses.'[4]

For these disgruntled journalists there was at least the circus and the theatres to offer distractions. At Hengler's circus there was a fairies' garden party and a coerced bear which 'goes through a series of manoeuvres on horseback whilst the horse is galloping round the ring. The bear leaps through rings and over poles with as much agility as an ordinary circus equestrian.'[5] At the Grand Theatre there was 'Cinderalla' and at the Prince of Wales Theatre 'Arabian Nights' – and Alice Leamar's sisters, Kate and Nelly, were dancing and singing at the Gaiety for 'an enormous salary'.[6] The sisters, who were staying at the Queen's Hotel with their two St.

[1] *South Wales Echo,* 14 May 1889.
[2] The *Dart,* 17 May 1889.
[3] The *Owl,* 15 March, 13 September 1889.
[4] Ibid., 10 May, 24 May 1889.
[5] The *Dart,* 3 May 1889.
[6] Ibid., 10 May 1889.

Bernard's dogs and a talking parrot, granted an audience to the *Dart,* which was buttered-up with the observation that Birmingham 'is beautifully improved ... Corporation Street is immense and so fashionable.'[7]

'The days are lengthening nicely, there's no football ... and whispers are getting louder about the beauties of Llandudno ...', a local newspaper reflected.[8] Just in time for the planning of the summer holidays, *Kirk's Holiday Guide; Or Where To Spend Your Holidays* appeared from the pen of the editor of the *Dart,* Robert Simpson Kirk. Free from 'boring ... historical and archaeological disquisitions' and written in 'a pleasant and gossipy way', the little book was crammed with information about travel, lodgings and other tips 'only picked up piecemeal over table d'hote or the promenade pipe'.[9] Priced at only sixpence, it was soon selling one thousand copies a week. Already some local residents were in Llandudno where, in 'lovely July-like weather', they listened to concerts on the pier, which was illuminated with electric light.[10] Reports also appeared of the delights to be found in the 'charming' Isle of Man, amongst them tennis, dancing – 'so much en vogue at Douglas' and 'open air concerts in ... fairy-like grounds.'[11]

Those without the money to spend the summer months in Llandudno or Bournemouth were not without distractions. On May Day Mitchell & Co. – purveyors of 'The standard shilling family ale' – organised their annual procession of decorated drays through the main streets of the city. This year the waggons were followed by a procession of children, organised by local Methodists, bearing such placards as 'But for drink we would be fed and clothed' and 'Father supports the drink'. The sight 'caused considerable comment.'[12] In front of 5,000 spectators Aston Villa managed to retain the Birmingham Challenge Cup by defeating Wolverhampton Wanderers 2-0. Very early one morning a prize

---

[7] Ibid.
[8] *Birmingham Saturday Night,* 1 June 1889.
[9] *Birmingham Daily Gazette,* 31 May 1889.
[10] The *Dart,* 31 May 1889.
[11] Ibid.
[12] *Derby Daily Telegraph,* 15 May 1889; *Birmingham Daily Post,* 2 May 1889. Henry Mitchell (1837-1913) founded his brewery in Smethwick in 1866; it merged with that of William Butler (1843-1907) in 1898.

fight was arranged just over the city boundary – the timing and location were intended to prevent interference by the police. For two hours, over sixty rounds, Sam Hill took on Lot Galeford in 'a most determined battle ... the men punishing each other with great severity.'[13] The purse was £20, divided at the end of the contest between the two men, much to the annoyance of some of Galeford's supporters.

With admission free and the local elite able to section themselves off in reserved one shilling seats, the town hall was filled to capacity for a lecture entitled 'The land for the people' by the American political economist Henry George, whose *Progress and Poverty* (1879) had become a best seller. The speaker sought 'to present arguments – not figures or mere theories', and at the conclusion of his speech the voting was unanimous, even local property owners pretending to agree with what was being said.[14] Also in the city was the itinerant phrenologist Mark Moores, who styled himself a professor and examined heads each morning and afternoon and gave lectures each evening. Another figure of interest this month was a sandwich board man traversing the main streets and seemingly capable of conversing in English, French, Spanish and Italian.

There was widespread concern in the city about the cattle market and slaughterhouses. There were about 300 slaughterhouses – many of them concentrated in an area of the city centre 'which no Birmingham man with a grain of self-respect would show to a stranger'.[15] Correspondents to the newspapers were troubled by both the issues of public health and the moral condition of working people. It was pointed out that the deep crevices in the floors of the slaughter houses meant that they could not easily be swilled and that the doors of slaughter houses were left open resulting in the slaughter man being seen from the road as he used an axe to dispatch the cattle: 'From morning to night, week after week', one correspondent lamented, 'men, women and children eagerly watch the process of slaughtering in its sickening details.'[16] Another situation irking the letter writers were naked young men immersing

---

[13] *South Wales Echo,* 20 May 1889.
[14] *Birmingham Daily Post,* 20 May 1889.
[15] Ibid., 2 May 1889.
[16] Ibid., 1 May 1889.

themselves in the canals and drying off by running and up and down the tow paths – whilst one shopkeeper, having lost 2000 cigars in a burglary and then seen enamelled letters prised off his shop window, wondered what exactly the police were doing.

Hospital Saturday was an ongoing collection in workplaces, begun in 1873, to provide funds for medical charities in the city. This month these efforts were supplemented when 'an army of ladies took possession of the corners of streets ...'[17] One young woman even jumped on and off omnibuses at Five Ways to secure donations. There was great satisfaction when these efforts brought the total sum for the year to £8000 – more than twice the sum raised a decade earlier. Doubtless less welcome was the news that the average age of death in Birmingham was 29.

[17] *Northampton Mercury,* 25 May 1889; *Birmingham Daily Post,* 17 May, 20 May 1889.

June

New Street railway station, opened in 1854, now entered its busiest period of the year. Middle class families set off for their holidays by the sea. The weather in Birmingham was 'dull, showery and cold', but Bournemouth, it was reported, was 'now looking at its best ... ablaze with rhododendrons ... (with) the temperature ... delightfully fresh and cool.'[1] The sea bathing was 'the best in England' and there were carriage drives to the New Forest and Corfe Castle (both six shillings return).[2] The 11.40 to Llandudno, arriving at 3.20, was packed most days. Staying at the Gwydyr Hotel – 'what puddings!' – or the Deganwy Castle Hotel – 'the view from the lawn is a picture' – or the West End Boarding House – where the tariff was two to three guineas with no additional charge for use of the bathrooms – or a myriad of other establishments, these 'thorough-going Llandudnites' were able to stroll along the promenade - now surfaced with asphalt rather than gravel - enjoy Punch and Judy shows, listen to musical performances on the pier and admire the aquatic skills of James Finney, a self-styled professor of swimming, and his sister Marie who appeared in the sea off the pier head every afternoon at 3.30.[3] There were also day excursions from New Street. One married man – unnamed in the press to spare his blushes – arranged to meet his new amour at the station for just such a jaunt. She was 'a prepossessing damsel who had just said goodbye to her teens', but, unfortunately, the couple were intercepted at the station by the man's wife; he legged it whilst she 'made short work of her rival's holiday finery ... ... leaving her to gather up what fragments were worth the trouble.'[4]

Some wealthier Brums decided to head across the English Channel to visit the exhibition in Paris. Across 237 acres, there was

---

[1] The *Dart,* 7 June, 14 June 1889.
[2] Ibid., 19 July 1889.
[3] Ibid., 14 June, 21 June, 12 July 1889. James Finney (1862-1924), a swimming instructor from Oldham, won numerous prizes in competitions across the north of England; his sister was noted for her diving, including from the pier in Llandudno.
[4] *Leicester Daily Mercury,* 22 June 1889.

art, architecture and new technology from around the world to inspect. For one visitor from Birmingham the experience turned out to be most unsatisfactory. On arrival he was offered a room at twenty francs – twice the going-rate – and then encountered the French police, 'the worst tempered body of men I ever came across.'[5] He was detained at the exhibition for refusing to pay an additional fee, and another police officer was summoned when he claimed that a boot cleaner was overcharging him. 'To save myself being locked up again', he ruefully recollected, 'I paid the money and went my way, with clean boots but with a very unclean temper.'[6] Though complaining about being charged five francs for two glasses of lemonade, another visitor found the visit more enjoyable, gazing at the newly-erected Eiffel Tower 'with the rays of the setting sun gleaming through it, giving it a weird, unearthly experience.'[7]

One man who was definitely detained in Birmingham was the councillor for Rotton Park Francis Clayton. Finally back from his foreign travels, he faced a by election in his ward because he had exceeded his permitted period of absence. His opponent was Joseph Tanner, one of a small band of supporters in the city of H.M. Hyndman's Social Democratic Federation. Tanner pressed home the case for the state ownership of the land, the mines and the railways, but he had little money and few workers and managed only to secure 160 votes against Clayton's 729.[8] Meanwhile the BCA acquired a new president, J. Satchell Hopkins; still sore from their failure to bring forward their man in the Central Birmingham by-election, the local Tories made clear that 'the Unionist alliance in Birmingham can only be satisfactorily renewed by the Conservatives receiving a fairer proportion of the parliamentary representation ...'[9]

The most stylish shops were located in New Street and Corporation Street. Locals and visitors filled the wooden pavements

---

[5] *Birmingham Daily Post,* 5 June 1889.
[6] Ibid.
[7] The *Dart,* 11 October 1889.
[8] S. Roberts, 'Independent Labour Politics in Birmingham, 1886-1914', *West Midlands Studies* (1983), 16, pp. 9-15. For a biographical sketch of the Quaker chemist Francis Clayton see *Faces and Places,* II, (1890), pp. 113-15.
[9] *Leicester Chronicle,* 29 June 1889.

as they made their way to Lewis' or the Grand Theatre. 'We won't trouble ourselves to attempt description of the comely matrons and maidens and their adornments', the *Dart* observed. 'Let bachelors, young and old, join the throng ...'[10] The only irritation were the throngs of cyclists - who themselves objected to the watering of the roads which greatly increased their chances of falling off their machines. Shopkeepers away from these fashionable streets complained that they were seeing little trade, and were also aggrieved by the horse fair, held every six months and described as 'a palpable and intolerable evil ... the filthy language we are compelled to listen to for the greater part of the day is enough to sicken one.'[11]

The parks of the city were extremely popular, visited by thousands each evening during the summer months. There were regular performances by bands; but in Victoria Park in Small Heath visitors complained about 'a perfect pandemonium' caused by children.[12] 'I beg to suggest that for the remainder of the season the musical instruments, bandstand and enclosure be given to the children entirely and the police band performers be allowed to wheel the perambulators and crying children on the walks outside', one disgruntled letter writer observed. 'The mixture of discord and operatic selections could not be more delightful any way and it would assist one to know whether it was intended for music or the onion fair.'[13] Also popular were the corporation baths in Northwood Street, though there were grumblings about 'the icy grip' of the water.[14] The police began to patrol Victoria Park, but decided there was nothing they could do about the temperature of the water in the baths.

Making the papers every month were reports of suicides and violent assaults, invariably described as 'shocking'. This month the most 'shocking' story concerned Elizabeth Coley, forced into

---

[10] The *Dart,* 28 June 1889.
[11] *Birmingham Daily Post,* 15 June, 18 June 1889.
[12] Ibid. For Victoria's visit to the park in March 1887, see C. Chinn, *Free Parks for the People* (Studley, 2012), pp. 66-7.
[13] *Birmingham Daily Post,* 5 June 1889. The onion fair did indeed sell onions as well as offering a range of amusements; it was moved out of the town centre in 1875.
[14] Ibid., 18 June 1889.

prostitution by Charles Rea, who then assaulted her with a poker; he was sentenced to six months' imprisonment with hard labour. The police court also broke up by the use of prison sentences two 'slogging gangs', groups of a dozen or more 'roughs' who threatened or used violence. Thomas Carroll was sentenced to six weeks with hard labour for pick pocketing – he was arrested the day after being released from Winson Green prison for the same offence. Thomas Brett was offered the choice of a fine of 15s. or fourteen days with hard labour for cutting his initials into a tree in a park. Betting was rife in public houses, which was in contravention of the Betting Act of 1853. The police organised several raids on pubs and arrested the culprits. One of these men, Adam Hicks, had taken 300 bets in three hours in the yard of the Justice Inn in Moor Street; he was fined £60.[15]

In Edgbaston Warwickshire County Cricket Club, founded in 1882, triumphed over Somerset, a 'magnificent catch' by Hugh Whitby causing much comment.[16] This was followed at the end of the month by a tennis tournament. Admission to 'one of the fashionable events of the year' cost two shillings and in 'grand weather ... some capital play ... (was) seen', notably by the Wimbledon champion Maud Watson who, in her final appearance at Edgbaston, won the three events she entered.[17]

'Why should not Birmingham have its bishop and so be a city in the fullest acceptation of the term?', one newspaper asked.[18] Plans were drawn up and meetings addressed, but it was to be another sixteen years before Birmingham became a diocese when Charles Gore arranged its separation from Worcester.[19]

[15] *South Wales Daily Echo,* 26 June 1889.
[16] The *Owl,* 28 June 1889. Hugh Whitby (1864-1934) was a fast bowler, best known for representing Oxford University.
[17] Ibid., 7 June, 21 June 1889. Maud Watson (1864-1946) won the ladies' singles at Wimbledon in 1884 and 1885
[18] *Northampton Mercury,* 22 June 1889; *Birmingham Daily Post,* 5 July, 9 July 1889.
[19] Charles Gore (1853-1932) became bishop of Worcester in 1901 and bishop of Birmingham in 1905.

July

The gentlemen amateurs of Warwickshire County Cricket Club were very busy, playing four matches this month. At Edgbaston large crowds gathered to see them take on Lancashire. When Warwickshire went into bat, 'it was very amusing to see how Birmingham faces lengthened as the local wickets fell like ninepins before the deliveries of Briggs and Watson'.[1] However, in their own bowling and fielding, Warwickshire acquitted themselves well, and 'little Albert Bird's beautiful catch from long-on fairly brought down the house'.[2] Lancashire won by five wickets, but Warwickshire had 'made a gallant fight of it ...'[3]

At the 'superbly-kept' Botanical Gardens open air dramatic and musical performances were put on, and the singing of Elsie Baugh won her admirers as her 'pleasant and full voice carried and was heard far and near'.[4] The number of excursions was described as 'almost bewildering'.[5] Brums could get the train to almost anywhere they fancied, some of them even opting for Helston in Cornwall, a journey which they discovered took fourteen hours. Less ambitiously, others decided to visit Kenilworth or Sutton Park or, in the case of the employees and their families of the New Street printer E.C. Osborne, Hampton-in-Arden, where they enjoyed 'a capital spread'.[6] A large party from the BMI – which had recently appointed the schoolmaster-poet Alfred Hayes as its new secretary – went by railway to Bridgnorth, where they took part in an 'exceptionally pleasant' six mile ramble.[7] At Bournbrook park things did not go so well. For the fourth time, George Higgins –

---

[1] The *Dart,* 26 July 1889. Johnny Briggs (1862-1902) was a highly-successful left-arm spin bowler; he was in devastating form against South Africa in 1888-9. Alexander Watson (1844-1920) was a slow bowler who played for Lancashire for twenty-four years.
[2] Ibid. Albert Bird (1867-1927) was a right-arm off-break bowler who subsequently played for Worcestershire.
[3] Ibid.
[4] Ibid., 5 July 1889.
[5] *Birmingham Daily Post,* 31 July 1889.
[6] The *Dart,* 12 July 1889.
[7] The *Owl,* 12 July 1889.

another man who drew attention to his particular expertise by styling himself 'professor' - and his assistant Emily De Voy cancelled a parachute jump from a hot air balloon, declaring that the wind was too strong. 'The parachutist was mobbed and assaulted', it was reported, 'and was only able to get away in a cab through the intervention of the police. His parachute was taken from him and torn to pieces'. Little wonder Higgins never returned to Birmingham.[8]

A visitor to Birmingham this month noted that the trams were 'abominably ugly but very convenient, except to the people they run over.'[9] Judging by the correspondence columns of the newspapers, these trams were often delayed and overcrowded. Brums were also disgruntled by industrial smoke ruining the 'choice' flowers and shrubs in their gardens and with their public fountains, too many of which were said to be out of order.[10] 'With a teetotal mayor', the *Dart* wondered, 'we might expect to have an abundance of water available for thirsty wayfarers.'[11] The mayor Richard Cadbury Barrow, however, had more than public fountains on his mind. He was immersed in arrangements for a visit to the city by the Shah of Persia.

Nasser Al Din, the Shah of Persia, had arrived in Britain in June. Having taken in the theatre, the opera, racing and garden parties, he arrived in Birmingham on 11 July to inspect factories. If an illustrious visitor wanted to do manufacturing, Birmingham was the go-to place. The Shah was two hours late when he arrived at New Street in the company of the British envoy to Teheran Sir Henry Drummond Wolff, having had a lie-in due to tiredness. Welcomed by the mayor, he boarded an open carriage and, with a military escort, proceeded through the main streets, calling in at the show rooms of the electro plate manufacturer George Elkington, before arriving at the Council House. Here the town clerk Edward Orford Smith, 'with many graceful bowings', read an address calling for stronger commercial ties between Britain and Persia - the Shah was so impressed by his display of obsequiousness, the *Dart* joked,

---

[8] *Leicester Daily Mercury,* 29 July 1889; *Birmingham Daily Post,* 15 July, 18 July 1889.

[9] *Penny Illustrated Paper,* 20 July 1889.

[10] *Birmingham Daily Post,* 26 July 1889.

[11] The *Dart,* 5 July 1889.

that he requested that Smith join his staff in Teheran.[12] Prepared to eat only hot food – a salmon on ice and frozen lobsters had to be removed from his table – for lunch the Shah then 'partook with much satisfaction to himself.'[13] In the afternoon visits were paid the factories of the glass manufacturer F. & C. Osler and of the Small Arms Company. The girls of Gillott's pen factory, dressed up for the occasion, were said to be very disappointed when a shortage of time prevented a visit. According to the newspapers, the people of Birmingham were delighted with the visit. Needless to say the satirical magazines saw it very differently:

> 'Then we looked at each other and said "Is that all?"
> Is that the great Shah – he's not handsome or tall;
> Was it really worthwhile then to make all this fuss?
> Pray what earthly good has his visit done us?
> So the men went to business – the boys to their schools;
> And we all seemed to think we'd been something like fools;
> While the flags were hauled down and the world went its way,
> Much the same as it does when the Shah stays away.[14]

The main beneficiaries in fact were the clothes and shoe shops in Corporation Street, heavily patronised by the Shah's entourage, and the enterprising cabbie who for the next few weeks attracted custom with the cry, "Who takes the Shah's cab?"[15]

The Birmingham Tories had by no means given up on their claim that their share of the parliamentary representation of Birmingham should be enlarged. At this point it stood at just one MP – Henry Matthews in East Birmingham. Lord Randolph Churchill was more than happy to oblige them in the fulfilment of this ambition, and duly arrived in the city at the end of the month. A garden party held at the home of the BCA President Sir James Sawyer was followed by a speech at the town hall in which Churchill, playing out the role of senior statesman, reviewed the situation in Europe and Ireland. He left no one in any doubt during this visit that he was willing to contest Birmingham again.

---

[12] The *Dart*, 19 July 1889.
[13] *Birmingham Faces and Places,* 1 August 1889.
[14] The *Dart*, 19 July 1889.
[15] Ibid.

Chamberlain made clear in private that he would not countenance it.[16] 'Joseph and Randolph together would be rather too much for one town or city', the *Dart* wryly observed.[17]

---

[16] R.F. Foster, *Lord Randolph Churchill* (Oxford, 1988), p. 357.
[17] The *Dart*, 26 July 1889.

August

On the first day of the month, after a long period of planning and preparation, an electrical and industrial exhibition opened at Bingley Hall; normally used for cattle sales, it had been transformed with 'the eye meet(ing) a stream of colour and light' and 'delightful fountains splashing crystal waters into basins.'[1] Lady Randolph Churchill was invited to officially open the exhibition, which her husband declared to be 'thoroughly worthy of the great city – the go-ahead city – in which it was held.'[2] Seeking to emulate the highly successful exhibition of manufactures held in the grounds of Bingley House forty years earlier, the exhibition was intended to be a showcase for the technological and industrial prowess of Birmingham. Such was the range of exhibits – from electric lighting and 'eerie' electrically-powered scales to telephones and musical instruments – that visitors could get around and look at things from an aerial railway.[3] A military band played during the day, and concerts with singers were organized in the evenings. It was reported that 9,000 people visited on the first day, paying 1s. admittance; a season ticket, which lasted for the three months' duration of the exhibition, could be purchased for 10s. 6d. The city council was not involved in the organisation, which was undertaken by a committee, with the brewer Joseph Ansell as chairman and T.C. Sharp as secretary. When the exhibition closed, it had taken £12,059 14s 5d in receipts and, after deducting expenses, had made a profit of £4,412. From this sum three Birmingham hospitals received £101. 7s. 2d. each. The remaining sum was absorbed by salaries and personal payments for the organisers, the exhibition being 'a commercial undertaking'; needless to say this provoked criticism in the newspapers.[4]

At the Crown Brewery, located behind the Crown Inn in Broad Street, the younger William Butler was taking a keen interest in the new electric lights. Already an electric lamp was installed in the yard, 'turning night into day'; and now an electric searchlight was

---

[1] The *Dart,* 9 August 1889.
[2] *Daily Gazette for Middlesbrough,* 3 August 1889.
[3] The *Dart,* 25 August 1889.
[4] *Birmingham Daily Post,* 22 May 1890, 7 April 1891.

erected on the roof.[5] With the equivalent power of 25,000 candles, it provoked strong reactions. There were complaints that by flashing on and off it disorientated passers-by and caused great disturbance. However, one journalist declared that it 'is all moonshine to think that it startles or frightens horses.'[6]

'The scene at the County Ground on Tuesday afternoon was worthy of the pencil of a Frith', the *Dart* observed. 'The members' pavilion was crowded with well-known citizens and patrons of cricket.'[7] It was the last match of the season, with Warwickshire taking on W.G. Grace's Gloucestershire. 'When Mr Bedford missed a very easy catch from Cranston, everybody was sorry for the tall and handsome son of the rector of Sutton', it was reported, 'and when, twenty minutes later, he caught the same batsman, everybody shouted for joy.'[8] The Warwickshire bowlers H.J. Pallett and J.E. Shilton won praise for taking four and three wickets respectively.[9] After making seven runs in the first innings, W.G. Grace was certainly wary of them, 'batt(ing) very carefully ... and never at all was he quite at home ...'[10] Though Gloucestershire won the match, it was recognised that Warwickshire had had a very good season, even if 'unreliability and funk are still characteristics.'[11]

It might have seemed like it in the members' pavilion at Edgbaston, but Birmingham was an industrial city. There were complaints of smoke from the chimneys in the Bull Ring, which led to goods outside shops being covered in soot: 'The nuisance goes on night and day.'[12] There was an outbreak of scarlet fever; by the end of the first week of August 269 children had been admitted to

---

[5] The *Dart,* 30 August 1889.

[6] *Birmingham Daily Post,* 19 August 1889; the *Dart,* 30 August 1889.

[7] Ibid., 16 August 1889. William Powell Frith (1819-1909) painted 'Derby Day' and 'The Railway Station', both of which depicted crowds.

[8] Ibid. William Kirkpatrick Riland Bedford (1826-1905) was rector of Sutton Coldfield for forty-two years. He was an antiquarian and also had a great interest in cricket and archery. William Campbell Riland Bedford (1852-1922) was also a clergyman and shared his father's sporting interests.

[9] Henry James Pallett (1863-1917) and John Edward Shilton were, respectively, right arm slow and left arm slow bowlers.

[10] The *Dart,* 16 August 1889.

[11] Ibid., 23 August 1889.

[12] Ibid., 2 August 1889.

hospital and, had the schools been open, the numbers would have been greater. There were stray dogs roaming the streets and the city council was soon catching, poisoning and cremating them 'at the rate of fifty a day.'[13] The fountain in Chamberlain Square, completed only nine years earlier, was in need of repair, and the *Dart* had what it regarded as some useful advice for the city council, pointing out that 'the average Brum could still just hang on to existence if the Chamberlain fountain was improved clean off the face of the earth.'[14] The Priory Works of E.V. Wilkes – which manufactured kettles, coal scoops and the like – was left 'completely gutted' by fire; the fire brigade were obstructed by the crowd 'and the hose pipes ... were wantonly cut by roughs, who also assaulted the police.'[15]

Many thousands of Brums were not in their home city at all, but at the seaside. So many in fact went to Llandudno at the start of the month that they were unable to find accommodation: '... hundreds were turned back to overrun Conway in search of beds, while some scores walked the streets all night or slept in railway carriages. Bathing vans were charged half-a-crown as bedrooms.'[16] Over the bank holiday weekend at the end of the month tens of thousands left on excursion trains from New Street or Snow Hill. Many travelled on the Saturday, but a number of these excursions left Birmingham between midnight on the Sunday and 3 a.m. on the Monday morning. And so on the actual bank holiday 5,300 Brums were to be found in North Wales, 3,600 in Scarborough, 3,200 in Blackpool, 1,200 in Weymouth, 1,100 in London, 1,005 in the Lake District, 900 in Liverpool and 250 in Southport.[17] Cheap as these day excursions were, they were still beyond the means of some working people. It was reported that 'some hundreds of the poorer classes who could not afford the railway

---

[13] *Carlisle Patriot,* 9 August 1889.
[14] The *Dart,* 23 August 1889. The previous month a bar maid, falsely accused of theft, had tried to drown herself in the Chamberlain fountain.
[15] *Cheltenham Chronicle,* 24 August 1889.
[16] The *Dart,* 9 August 1889.
[17] This topic is well-explored in S. Major, *Early Victorian Railway Excursions* (Barnsley, 2015).

fares started out in the middle of the night preceding the bank holiday to their favourite resorts.'[18]

For those who did not go for a day at the seaside, there were other things to do that bank holiday. Those who fancied spending the day fishing took advantage of cheap trips by rail to Sutton Park and Stratford-upon-Avon. At Aston Park there was a cycling competition, with prizes amounting to £250; strong men and trapeze artists also performed. In the grounds of Moor Green Hall there was a flower show, and in the grounds of Moseley Hall a temperance rally, featuring athletics and brass bands as well as speeches.

A significant development took place at the Hope Street Baptist Chapel in Highgate. Peter Thomas Stanford became pastor. He had arrived in the city from Bradford in 1885 and his appointment as pastor met with 'violent opposition' from some local Baptists.[19] Allegations in a letter from a Baptist minister of 'abominable wickedness' on his part had to be investigated and disproved.[20] Stanford's stipend was simply what was left over from the pew rents and collections after expenses had been paid. Born the son of slaves in Virginia, USA, Stanford was the first black pastor in Birmingham. He was a talented preacher and significantly increased membership of the chapel. It was not, however, 'altogether a bed of roses ... He had not only to put up with the opposition of foes, but the insincerity of those who should have stood shoulder to shoulder with him ... Mr Stanford's colour had been of no help to him in religious circles in the city ...'[21] With its membership growing, the chapel moved to new premises in Priestley Road, but Stanford's plan to build an even larger chapel named after William Wilberforce came to nothing.[22] When he set off for the USA to investigate lynching in 1895 – having been presented with an inscribed fountain pen, a musical box and other

---

[18] Ibid., 16 August 1889.
[19] *Sheffield Telegraph,* 29 August 1889.
[20] *Birmingham Daily Post,* 10 February 1892.
[21] Ibid., 19 December 1893.
[22] Ibid., 21 March 1891, 26 May, 29 November, 1 September, 6 December 1892.

items by his admirers - it was with the intention of eventually returning to Britain but he never did.[23]

Almost unnoticed a favourite son returned to Brum. He was W.J. Davis, the secretary of the Amalgamated Society of Brassworkers. Amongst the very first working class representatives on the school board and town council in Birmingham, Davis had been employed as a factory inspector in Sheffield. The *Dart* saw in him a challenger to the Chamberlain hegemony:

Lo! From dirty Sheffield yonder,
Davis is home to come;
Absence makes the heart grow fonder,
He'll be welcome back in Brum ...
Here is food for Brum's digestion,
Something rather spicy sweet;
Matthews and the eastern question
W.J. Davis fighting his seat.[24]

In the event W.J. Davis was a Lib-Lab candidate not in East Birmingham in 1892, but in Bordesley. He was defeated by Jesse Collings.[25]

---

[23] Ibid., 25 July, 2 October, 24 November 1894. Stanford died in 1909. See P. Walker, 'The Revd. Thomas Stanford (1860-1909): Birmingham's "coloured preacher"' (Ph.D. thesis, University of Manchester, 2004).
[24] The *Dart,* 23 August 1889.
[25] Collings: 6380; Davis 2658.

September

The lure of the seaside was still strong in Birmingham. In Bournemouth Brums were amongst a mile-long line of cyclists who, with their paper lanterns, looked 'like a long fiery serpent'.[1] Back in the city, the 'everlasting grumbling' continued in the correspondence columns of the newspapers – about the trams, the rubbish in Corporation Street, the stench at Snow Hill, the price of bread, the use by youths of catapults ('as effective as a small revolver') and the wages of junior clerks, with an employer paying only 7s a week 'thoroughly deserv(ing) ... to be robbed by his employees'.[2]

For six successive nights at the Prince of Wales the celebrated comic actor J.L. Toole was 'in his best form' as he reprised his popular characters such as Paul Pry.[3] If that wasn't enough, the following week the theatre offered a production of 'The Balloon', described by the *Owl* as 'the liveliest, jolliest, roaringest, screamingest piece of foolery of its sort ever produced ...'[4] Wombell's Travelling Menagerie – which transported lions, bears, wolves, monkeys and other animals in cages around the country – meanwhile arrived at Aston. Whilst his cage was being cleaned out, one of the lions escaped, the keeper 'momentarily diverted by a fight between an ostrich and a deer.'[5] There was 'a scene of wild confusion', but the 'bewildered' lion was recaptured after being driven into a sewer by 'Mustang Ned, our elephant subjugator'.[6] A second lion then made a break for it, staying loose throughout the night. 'Now just fancy how comfortable I would have felt when

---

[1] The *Dart*, 13 September 1889.
[2] *Birmingham Daily Post*, 26 September, 27 September, 28 September 1889. The *Dart*, 4 October 1889, had no sympathy for clerks, describing them as 'empty-headed with only mechanical brains.'
[3] *Birmingham Daily Post*, 21 September 1889. John Lawrence Toole (1830-1906) was encouraged to become a professional comic by Charles Dickens in the early 1850s and went on to enjoy a long career, culminating in a tour of Australia and New Zealand in 1890.
[4] The *Owl*, 27 September 1889.
[5] *Gloucester Citizen*, 28 September 1889.
[6] Ibid; *Birmingham Daily Post*, 2 October 1889.

going down the Aston Road on Saturday morning', a correspondent who left for work in the early hours wrote, 'if I had known that a lion was likely to pounce upon me at any minute.'[7]

The football season began again. Aston Villa met their old adversaries Preston North End in the third match of the season. The Villa had begun the season inauspiciously, whilst Preston 'in their first League match had thrashed Stoke with a roughness and a vigour that seemed to bode ill for most other clubs in that organisation.'[8] At Perry Barr, however, Preston 'met their masters in all departments of the game', Villa winning 5-3.[9] There was, the *Dart* observed, 'good stuff in the team ... Archie Hunter is a king of players ... a marvel for judgement in the field.'[10] Villa then promptly lost 3-0 to West Bromwich Albion, who this season had already impressively dispatched Notts County 2-1. Small Heath meanwhile took on Walsall Town Swifts 'and, after a series of scrambles in which there was quite enough display of temper, a draw of one goal each was the result'.[11]

At Selly Oak a prize fight took place for a stake of £5 took place between Alf Bayliss and George Coley. It was a short contest, Coley being knocked out after twenty-four minutes. 'No police were present', it was reported, 'but news reached the scene of the encounter that they were coming and a stampede ensued ... leaving the principals to get home as best they could'[12]

As ever, the police court in Moor Street was fully occupied. Each morning three magistrates brought to a conclusion lesser offences, referring the serious charges to the Birmingham Assizes. Brums before the magistrates found themselves fined for dodging railway fares (1s.), using obscene language in the main thoroughfares (2s. 6d.) or keeping a brothel (£5). Assaults resulted in imprisonment with hard labour. Elizabeth Chillingworth, a prostitute, was punished with 21 days with hard labour for assaulting

---

[7] Ibid., 1 October 1889. The *Dart*, 4 October 1889 relates a third disaster when the wind blew over several of the vans containing the animals, injuring many of them.
[8] *Birmingham Daily Post*, 23 September 1889.
[9] Ibid.
[10] The *Dart*, 27 September 1889.
[11] Ibid.
[12] *Birmingham Daily Post*, 16 September 1889.

a police constable (not an uncommon offence in Birmingham). A large number of people were repeatedly convicted for being drunk and disorderly. When the magistrate informed John Giblin that he had seen him before, he received the reply 'we always meet at the same old spot' – Giblin had 54 previous convictions and, on this occasion, was fined 10s.[13] Billy Poole made his 140th appearance before the magistrates and was fined 10s; he claimed the police were 'down on him if ever he had a glass of ale.'[14]

The local politicians were warming up for the forthcoming municipal elections. Joe made a big speech at the town hall, seeking to tempt some of his old Liberal allies into the Unionist embrace. 'Highbury has ordered the elimination of every Gladstonian from the city council', the *Dart* reported. 'Not a fragment shall be left.'[15]

---

[13] *Birmingham Daily Post,* 3 September 1889.
[14] Ibid., 6 September 1889.
[15] The *Dart,* 13 September 1889.

October

Bazaars were a popular form of fund-raising, particularly by churches. A public hall would be transformed into a medieval scene or a foreign city by a scenic artist and visitors would pay sixpence to get in. A number of bazaars were organised to help pay off the building costs of St. Alban's Church in Highgate, which opened in 1881. This month Curzon Hall was turned into 'Venice ... The Best Scenic Effect Ever Produced in the Provinces'.[1] The *Dart* very much enjoyed its visit: 'The scenery is magnificent ... the costumes gorgeous ... the orchestra ... simply screaming fun.'[2] Meanwhile Vesta Tilley was back in the city. 'The audience never seem to tire of her', it was reported, 'and six or seven songs and as many curtains are demanded before she is allowed to quit the boards.'[3]

At Perry Barr Aston Villa supporters often saw their team triumph. This month Villa defeated Derby County 7-1 at home – a result achieved either because the team 'played with great dash and brilliance' or because of the referee, who Derby unsuccessfully sought to change at half time.[4] It was a different story away from home – a truth amply demonstrated by a 7-0 'smashing up' at Blackburn Rovers.[5] The team was not helped by an ongoing dispute between the committee and some of the players – on one occasion the goal keeper Jimmy Warner, a key member of the team, refused to play.[6] A local reporter made no attempt to hide with annoyance at the inconsistent form of Villa, 'the most exasperating organisation the football public has ever known.'[7] For West Bromwich Albion two defeats followed in succession: 5-0 to Preston North End and then 4-1 to Wolverhampton Wanderers, in which 'some of the men

---

[1] *Birmingham Daily Post,* 17 October 1889.
[2] The *Dart,* 4 October 1889.
[3] Ibid., 18 October 1889.
[4] *Birmingham Daily Post,* 14 October 1889.
[5] Ibid., 21 October 1889.
[6] Jimmy Warner (1865-1943) played for Aston Villa for six seasons, appearing in the F.A. Cup finals of 1887 and 1892, leaving after the latter to join the Manchester club Newton Heath.
[7] *Birmingham Daily Post,* 21 October 1889.

performing were comparatively useless'.[8] At least Small Heath, in pouring rain, managed a 2-2 draw with Sheffield Wednesday.

The Guardians of the Poor managed the relief of the poor. There were sixty of these gentlemen, elected every three years. They did not receive remuneration. There was an outcry, however, when it was reported that at one workhouse meeting there had been 'most extravagant' expenditure on refreshments.[9] The newspaper correspondents strongly objected to 'their mighty efforts in the feeding ... and in the drinking line', declaring 'it is monstrous that such scenes should be enacted in the presence of paupers'.[10] It was recalled by one letter-writer that, at Selly Oak workhouse, he had witnessed 'dish after dish of savoury viands ... being removed' and by another how these men had 'regaled themselves with such splendour and extravagance at the ratepayers expense in the celebrated Scotch tour in search of a matron ...'[11] In reply it was stated that there had been no such tour and that refreshments at meetings did not extend beyond 'but two plain joints on the table', but to no avail: those who had enjoyed the repast that had begun the controversy managed to keep their identities private but ended up footing the bill of £11. 19s 7d themselves.[12]

The supply of gas had been a municipal enterprise since 1875. The price had been reduced from 3s. 1d. at the time of municipalisation to 2s. 3d. in 1889. The city council also sold gas stoves and gas appliances. There were, however, a growing number of complaints about gas lights – which were dim in comparison to electric lights – and gas fires. 'I am the unhappy proprietor of one of these inventions', one correspondent noted, 'and, when I light it in the morning, I am obliged to go to a coal fire in another room to get warm'.[13] Another correspondent observed that the street lights were brighter in other cities and that he was unable to read or write until later in the evening when the shops closed and the gas pressure increased. The *Dart* could be relied upon to have an

---

[8] Ibid.
[9] Ibid., 12 October 1889.
[10] Ibid., 18 October 1889.
[11] Ibid., 12 October, 18 October.
[12] Ibid., 19 October 1889. The five gentlemen offered their resignations, but these were refused.
[13] Ibid., 12 October 1889.

opinion about something so closely associated with its arch-enemy: 'It was a huge mistake, that purchase of gas', it tartly observed. 'Can't we sell the gas concern to a private company and, if there is a loss, ask Joe to make it up?'[14]

By the last week of the month, in the five wards where there was to be a contest in the municipal elections, posters had liberally been pasted up on walls and nightly meetings and canvassing were being organised. For the Unionists, ignoring almost entirely local matters, this was to be an effort to vanquish the Gladstonians and the cause of Irish Home Rule. For their opponents it was about 'class exclusion', of getting working class representatives off the city council – three of the Liberal candidates were leading Lib-Labs.[15] The greatest attention was focused on St. Thomas' ward, where twenty-six year old Austen Chamberlain was making his political debut. Chamberlain had long understood that his father intended him for a political career, and he approached the contest with confidence and arrogance. He revealed before the election that he intended to serve on the gas committee. 'The city was really a company', Chamberlain observed. 'He had nothing to say against working men representatives; but would shareholders appoint a man who had no leisure and was in no way educated to deal with large concern?'[16] His opponent was the secretary of the Amalgamated Tinplate Workers' Association J.V. Stevens, described as having 'a vandalistic pleasure in smashing up an opponent. He hits hard and does not foam if hit back.'[17] Stevens declared that Chamberlain was relying on the family name and branded him 'a bitter enemy of the working classes'.[18] Presented as 'a working man himself, working day by day at his trade in St. Thomas' ward', Stevens was reported to have 'created a capital impression and many Tories will vote for him.'[19] These 'many Tories' had clearly not forgotten the shabby way in which they had been treated by Joseph Chamberlain over Central Birmingham.

---

[14] The *Dart*, 18 October 1889.
[15] *Birmingham Daily Post*, 31 October 1889.
[16] Ibid., 29 October 1889.
[17] Quoted in J. M. Bellamy and J. Saville eds. *Dictionary of Labour Biography* (1974), II, p. 358.
[18] *Birmingham Daily Post*, 30 October 1889.
[19] The *Owl*, 18 October 1889.

Austen Chamberlain also graced the voters of Bordesley and Duddeston with visits. In Bordesley Eli Bloor, an organizer in his own trade of glass making, was the Lib-Lab candidate. First elected to represent the ward in 1883, he had successfully pressed for a reduction in the hours of work of gas workers. 'It is quite possible', he added in response to Chamberlain's assertions that men like him made the most suitable councillors, 'that some representatives of labour were as equal to the task as young gentlemen who matriculated at college.'[20] He made sure working men addressed his meetings. Bloor's Unionist rival James Moffat was a self-made businessman in the building trade, and was therefore, in his own estimation, 'in every sense a labour candidate.'[21] The Lib-Lab candidate in St. George's ward was the former Chartist James Whateley, who faced a Tory nominee T. Emory Davies. A councillor for eighteen years Whatley 'was modest in all that he said about himself and Mr Davies was – well, the reverse.'[22] In Nechells the tiny but persistent branch of the Social Democratic Federation brought forward Joseph Tanner to challenge the Liberal incumbent J.T. Middlemore. Deeply irritating to the BLA, he claimed he was offered money not to stand. It was claimed that the Liberal candidate in Duddeston W.L. Barber was 'loved by his employees'; 'bosh' shouted a voice from the crowd.[23]

---

[20] *Birmingham Daily Post,* 31 October 1889.
[21] Ibid., 25 October 1889.
[22] Ibid., 2 November 1889.
[23] Ibid., 1 November 1889.

November

The outcome of the municipal elections for Joseph Chamberlain and the Liberal Unionists was 'an ignominious defeat all along the line.'[1] In the five contested wards the Liberal candidates were all returned.[2] Stevens' victory over Austen Chamberlain, albeit by a narrow majority, was completely unexpected. 'His self-wisdom was too apparent', the *Dart* observed, 'and his crude lectures to workmen on their relative position to their employers were certain to provoke antagonism'.[3] It was, however, the defection of Tory burgesses to Stevens' cause, the magazine believed, that caused the upset:

> Joseph Chamberlain said what he'd do,
> But was lax in performing his promises;
> So the Tories have squirmed a bit too late,
> And Austen is out for St. Thomas' ...
> The affair has exactly turned out,
> As once Joseph Rowlands predicted,
> He must love this Gladstonian shout,
> And the groans of the party evicted.
> He chuckles no doubt at the fate
> Of the son of the man he once trusted
> To put in a new boiler plate
> Which was rotten and so the thing's busted.[4]

The Liberals was thrilled by the results: 'Collings is doomed in Bordesley and Matthews marked for political death in East Birmingham ... this may be the beginning of the end.'[5]

---

[1] The *Dart,* 8 November 1889.
[2] St. Thomas's: J.V. Stevens 1301, A. Chamberlain 1290; Bordesley: E. Bloor 2965, J. Moffat 1790; St. George's: J. Whateley 1514, T. Emery Davies 978; Duddeston: W.L. Barber, 1423, F. Lowe 1138; Nechells: J.T. Middlemore 1059, J. Tanner 427.
[3] The *Dart,* 8 November 1889.
[4] The *Dart,* 8 November 1889.
[5] The *Owl,* 8 November 1889; the *Dart,* 8 November 1889.

Tory votes for Stevens was described by one supporter as 'a senseless and miserable policy of revenge.'[6] An attempt was made to repair the strained relations between the Liberal Unionists and the Conservatives at a meeting at the Queen's Hotel in Stephenson Street. At this meeting, Joseph Chamberlain made clear that the existing arrangements for parliamentary representation – with six of the seven constituencies allocated to Liberal Unionists – should be preserved. For the Tories J. Satchell Hopkins demanded that two of the Unionist candidates should be from their party. With a great deal of ill feeling and no agreement, the matter was referred to the Unionist leadership in London.[7]

The *Owl* meanwhile found itself threatened with being sued for libel by the secretary of the Birmingham Liberal Unionists, James Skuse Baily. The magazine had drawn attention to the employment by Baily of the Revd. A.F. Barfield as a Liberal Unionist lecturer. A Walsall Congregationalist minister, Barfield had achieved notoriety by disappearing in the company of twenty-year old Maggie Bourne, a member of his congregation, leaving behind his wife and seven children.[8] Skuse declared that he had suspected nothing untoward about Barfield, but the *Owl* saw the threat of legal action as a nakedly political attack with the aim of shutting down the magazine. 'So the renegade Liberals would like to stop the *Owl* would they?', its editor William Byron Smith declared. 'Mr Chamberlain is a big man, but we are not afraid of him.'[9] In the event Baily did not proceed with legal action.

Joseph Chamberlain's opponents had long criticized his interest 'in dazzling schemes for beautiful streets':[10]

> We dubbed it the acme of absurdity,
> And objected to throw away millions;
> It's been a dear bargain, there can be no doubt,
> And we say it without hesitation,
> It's a drain on our means we could well be without,

---

[6] *Birmingham Daily Post,* 1 November 1889.
[7] S. Roberts, *Sir Benjamin Stone 1838-1914: Photographer, Traveller and Politician* (Birmingham, 2014), pp.47-9.
[8] *Birmingham Daily Post,* 25 September, 27 September 1889.
[9] The *Owl,* 15 November 1889.
[10] The *Dart,* 22 November 1889.

Is this boulevard of the Corporation.[11]

The Tory-supporting *Birmingham Daily Gazette* decided to employ an investigative journalist R. Lewis James to write a series of reports on the other side of Birmingham. He painted a grim picture of slum life: 'There are courts in the very centre of Birmingham where filth accumulates on filth ... where courtyards are so many acres of stink ... where doorless privies face house doors and make decency impossible ... where it is a danger for a police man to enter after dark.'[12] The fear of crime provoked a public debate about the lighting of these courts, of which there were estimated to be 6,000. What had to be decided was whether the landlords or the city council should take meet the costs.

Still there was the theatre to take minds off this weighty question. The Grand marked its seventieth anniversary with productions of 'Doris', an opera, and 'Sweet Lavender', a comedy; its proprietor Andrew Melville was declared to be 'one of the best known and most popular men in the city.'[13] At the Prince of Wales 'Little Lord Fauntleroy' being put on, with Vera Beringer and C.W. Somerset in the leading roles. The comedian Dan Leno was delivering his ramblings at the Gaiety.[14] Amateur performers were also treading the boards, putting on 'The Rivals' at the assembly rooms in Edgbaston which were 'filled to overflowing with a fashionable and distinguished audience.'[15] The Midland Conservative Club meanwhile enjoyed a smoking concert, forgetting about Joe for a while and enjoying the comic songs of Hubert Langford. Greatly in demand as an entertainer, Langford also performed this month at a dinner organised by the Centaur Cycling Club at the Great Western Hotel.

There remained a considerable appetite for visits by phrenologists in Birmingham. At the Exchange Rooms in New

---

[11] Ibid., 13 December 1889.

[12] *Birmingham Daily Gazette,* 22 November 1889.

[13] Ibid., 15 November 1889. Andrew Melville (1853-1896) and his family owned theatres across the country.

[14] Dan Leno (1860-1904) was the stage name of George Galvin. At first a singer and dancer, he later concentrated on patter, humorously describing ordinary people and situations.

[15] The *Dart,* 15 November 1889.

Street there was free admission - with reserved seats available for 1s. - to the lectures of Arthur Cheetham on such matters as 'Faces and how to read them' and 'Courtship and marriage'.[16] Arrangements were made for admission of women and men on different evenings, and the audiences were able to 'go home with the conviction that phrenology is an indisputable science and not a sham or a snare ...'[17] Private consultations during the day for heads to be read and for treatment with Cheetham's 'electro curative battery' were also available.[18] No sooner had Cheetham left, than L.N. Fowler and his daughter Jessie arrived.[19]   Heads were examined and lectures delivered at the Masonic Hall in Severn Street on 'How to rise in the world' and 'Love, courtship and marriage.' For those more interested in growing chrysanthemums than character analyses, there was an extensive exhibition of these plants at the town hall.

A 2-1 Aston Villa victory against Wolverhampton Wanderers at the beginning of the month was marred by a stone being thrown at one of the opposition players; a £5 reward was offered for information identifying the culprit. This month saw three successive defeats for Aston Villa. 'The cause of the defeat', it was reported after Villa lost 2-1 to Everton at Perry Barr, 'lay in the raggedness and slovenliness - at time almost amounting to incompetency - exhibited in the vanguard.[20] There was talk of new players being brought in. At Stoney Lane West Bromwich defeated Burnley 2-1, 'dashing down the slope, slipping the ball from toe-to-toe with dazzling precision and closing around goal furiously and relentlessly.'[21] Unfortunately, this was followed by a 5-0 defeat at Blackburn Rovers. Small Heath meanwhile continued to implement their policy of securing draws.

---

[16] Arthur Cheetham (1864-1937) later became a noted film maker, in 1898 becoming the first man to film a football match.

[17] The *Dart*, 8 November 1889.

[18] Ibid.

[19] Lorenzo Niles Fowler (1811-96) was American-born, arriving in Britain in 1863; he undertook numerous lecture tours and wrote extensively to promote phrenology.

[20] *Birmingham Daily Post*, 25 November 1889.

[21] Ibid.

December

Mayor Clayton's idea of taking his Corporation on a trot round the vile, unlighted courts of the city is a good one', the *Dart* observed.[1] One councillor, believing that he was visiting an area in his own ward, distributed sweets to the children he encountered; others concluded that 'they would rather not live there.'[2] One correspondent declared that, if the city council reduced the cost of installing pipes, he was prepared to light the courts attached to the houses he owned. The town clerk Edward Orford Smith expressed the view that, using powers granted under Artisans' Dwellings Act of 1875, the city council could force property owners to light the courts. It was believed that the gas lamps would be in place by the following winter, though before that 'those lucky fellows, the lawyers, will pocket some fees and do much talking.'[3]

The pantomimes were returning to the theatres of Birmingham. At the Prince of Wales there was 'Cinderella' and at the Grand 'Puss in Boots'. The Theatre Royal put on 'Aladdin', featuring 'satirical local allusions.'[4] The notorious dinner eaten by several of the Poor Law Guardians was amongst these local references:

Aladdin: I'm ready for a revision committee's feast – all that's in season, regular workhouse fare.
Widow Twankey: We're quickly served.
Aladdin: A banquet, I declare.
Ben: (presenting menu): Fish, lamb, ducks, grouse – any shrimps?
Aladdin: Go on, call over.
Ben: Salmon, lobsters, leverets.
Widow Twankey: We are in clover.
Ben: Will you drink water?
Widow Twankey: I never go to that length.
Ben: Beer, wine, spirits.

---

[1] The *Dart,* 20 December 1889.
[2] Ibid.
[3] Ibid., 27 December 1889; *Morning Post,* 17 December 1889.
[4] *Birmingham Daily Post,* 20 December 1889.

Aladdin: Ah, Union is strength.
Ben: Desert is provided – also three pints of cream.
Widow Tankey: Excels a gormandising Guardian's dream.[5]

For one night a dramatic cantata entitled 'The Maid of Astolat', inspired by the writings of Sir Thomas Malory and Alfred Lord Tennyson and composed by Birmingham-born organist Charles Swinnerton Heap, was performed at the town hall. Despite featuring a 450-strong chorus, the attendance fell below expectations and money was lost.[6] Rather more modestly, the Midland Railway Band performed at Gem Street Board School and 'the songs of Tom Burrows particularly delighted his audience'; there was also a concert by the ladies' singing class of the Birmingham and Midland Institute.[7] It was reported that the organ at St. Paul's Church, built in 1790, had been refurbished 'and ... is once again in magnificent form.'[8]

The correspondence columns continued to bring out the best, and the worst, in Brums. The proposal by city council to construct a winter garden and exhibition hall in Corporation Street was met with counter proposals, amongst them a barracks for the Salvation Army and a structure resembling the Eiffel Tower; replying to this second idea, a correspondent suggested a lunatic asylum 'for the use of the authors of the wild suggestions we are having at the moment.'[9] In spite of numerous petitions, the city council went ahead with their plans for an exhibition hall. There were other things to complain about – the lack of direction signs on omnibuses and trams, 'the most sickening odour' from the drains in Edgbaston, the dim clock at New Street station which was 'wretchedly illuminated by a single jet in front of instead of behind the face' and the failure of wealthier residents and the city council to

---

[5] Ibid., 26 December 1889.
[6] Charles Swinnerton Heap (1847-1900) was educated at King Edward's School and Cambridge and was a familiar figure on the Birmingham music scene. He was a friend of Edward Elgar. This composition is no longer performed.
[7] The *Dart,* 13 December 1889.
[8] Ibid., 27 December 1889.
[9] *Birmingham Daily Post,* 3 December 1889.

clear snow from the footpaths in front of their properties.[10] It was pointed out that 'in Birmingham, in this respect at any rate, there is one law for the rich and another for the poor and that the corporation includes themselves among the rich.'[11] The Birmingham-born radical journalist George Jacob Holyoake observed that there were not enough street signs in 'my own city': 'Birmingham is a manufacturing city and it could in a week cast street plates enough for all the cities of the world ... Birmingham is a commercial city; you invite the customer to it ... but the stranger who cannot pay for a cab is soon lost in the streets ...'[12]

There were a large number of brothels in Birmingham. In general the police did not interfere with these, unless there were complaints from neighbours or another offence was being committed on the premises. For a first offence, brothel-keepers were fined £5. Annie Lowe of New Canal Street found herself before the magistrates when she enticed a man into her house, and his watch and chain were stolen. The police constable who was called to the brothel 'found three women and two men in one bed.'[13] Lowe was sentenced to three months with hard labour. This month the magistrates also fined two omnibus drivers 10s. each for racing each other along New Street, and a passenger also had to forfeit 10s. when he used obscene language on an omnibus. John Viney, aged eighty-five and evidently of an artistic bent, was fined 5s. after entering a public house, drawing some sketches and becoming intoxicated after customers 'gave him two glasses of very nice beer and called him Father Christmas.'[14]

Heavy snow fell in Birmingham this month. An enterprising businessman from Rhyl wrote to say that they were 'enjoying a perfect summer ... with an air so gentle that even our veterans of eighty could be seen sunning themselves ... We have ... every possible means of promoting health and of fortifying our fortunate

---

[10] Ibid., 11 December, 12 December 1889.
[11] Ibid., 3 December 1889.
[12] Ibid., 12 December 1889. George Jacob Holyoake (1817-1906) championed freethought and co-operation, and edited and contributed to numerous periodicals, most notably the *Reasoner*.
[13] Ibid., 17 December 1889.
[14] Ibid., 24 December 1889.

midlanders against the Russian catarrh which is defying doctors.'[15] The Barmouth Hotel advertised itself as a 'splendid winter resort', and the readers of the *Dart* were able to enter a competition to win a fortnight in either Llandudno or Aberystwyth.[16] 'Preference will be given to a newly-married couple', the editor informer potential entrants.[17]

When players succumbed to illness, Small Heath struggled to field eleven players, but this month enjoyed 'a rare fillip' by defeating Walsall Town Swifts 4-0.[18] However, a 'severe drubbing' followed, as they lost 9-1 to Sheffield Wednesday.[19] West Bromwich Albion were on a losing streak and recruited two new players from Scotland; this clearly revitalized them as a 4-1 victory against Accrington Stanley was followed by a 2-2 draw with Preston North End. This month Aston Villa played four matches in one week, including one on Christmas Day, drawing one and losing three. As the players left the pitch after the 1-1 draw with Wolverhampton Wanderers, they were pelted with mud and two players were assaulted, though one of them 'gave his assailant a good deal of interest in the few rapid exchanges that took place.'[20] The performance in the 3-2 defeat against Preston North End won praise, but, against Derby County, 'a demoralised team, which had by this time arrived at the stage which is known as "sixes and sevens" went under very easily', losing 5-0.[21]

It did not get any better for Aston Villa during the rest of the season. The new year began with a 7-0 defeat by Everton. 'They went away with the certainty of defeat staring them in the face – and they got it in a fashion which will probably disgust many of those who so far have always been anxious to find excuses for them', it was reported. 'It is pitiful to see the name of the club being made a laughing stock ...'[22] At the end of the season the club only avoiding re-election to the Football League because they tallied in fourth

---

[15] Ibid., 20 December 1889; *Dundee Courier,* 23 December 1889.
[16] *Birmingham Daily Post,* 25 December 1889.
[17] The *Dart,* 27 December 1889.
[18] *Birmingham Daily Post,* 9 December 1889.
[19] Ibid., 23 December 1889.
[20] Ibid.
[21] Ibid., 30 December 1889.
[22] Ibid., 6 January 1890.

place from the bottom with Bolton Wanderers. Yet a golden era lay ahead – in 1894 Aston Villa won the Football League and repeated the feat in 1896, 1897, 1899 and 1900, as well as winning the F.A. Cup in 1895 and 1897. Small Heath were promoted to the First Division in 1894. That October, in front of 15,000 spectators, they held Aston Villa 2-2. In 1905 Small Heath changed their name to Birmingham Football Club.

Driving his horse and cart through the streets of Birmingham the pedlar William Poole was a familiar figure to local people – and indeed also to the magistrates. He was known to all as Billy Poole. When he was arrested for being drunk and disorderly this month, he broke down in tears and claimed that he 'had been going along all right, having only had two cups of beer, which were given him by a gentleman.' [23] The police confirmed that Billy 'had behaved very well this year'.[24] On this occasion he was sent away without punishment. Billy was frequently before the magistrates for being drunk and disorderly – so often that the authorities lost count of the number of occasions they had dealt with him, the highest estimate being 170 times. He was periodically imprisoned, as in 1892 when he was sentenced in March and again in May to one month with hard labour. 'He is a disgrace to the city', an exasperated magistrate declared. 'I don't know what we can do with him. He is seventy years old and it is a marvel that he is alive. I suppose it is only prison that saves his life.'[25] It is unlikely that Billy ever made it to Llandudno.

---

[23] Ibid., 30 December 1889.
[24] Ibid.
[25] Ibid., 5 March 1892; ibid., 16 June 1893.

Illustrations

fth Year, No. 253. **THE DART.** *Friday, August 26, 1881.*

MR. E. ORFORD SMITH.
(Town Clerk of Birmingham.)

Edward Orford Smith. Employed as town clerk from 1881 until 1907, it was his idea to mark the fiftieth anniversary of the charter of incorporation by securing city status for Birmingham.

The *Owl*, which despised Joseph Chamberlain, suggests that the motto for Birmingham should not be 'Forward' but 'Backward.' Chamberlain and an unflattering representation of the de Bermingham family stand either side of the shield, which in its centre depicts 'Squirt Square' – the Chamberlain fountain.

The Central Birmingham by-election in April 1889. The Liberal Unionist Albert Bright, the son of the recently-deceased and much-revered John Bright, is depicted on the left and his Liberal challenger Phipson Beale is depicted on the right. Bright was resoundingly returned.

AFTER THE SHAH.

THE MAYOR.—Good Gracious, Orful! what's the matter with your back ?
THE TOWN CLERK.—You can't expect me to walk straight after last week's genuflexions

When the Shah of Persia visited Birmingham in July 1889, the town clerk Edward Orford Smith bowed to him several times, much to the amusement of the satirical magazines. The mayor Richard Cadbury Barrow is also depicted here.

Austen Chamberlain sought a seat on the city council in November 1889, and appears here as an arrogant-looking young man alongside his smug-looking father. The two men are depicted as orchids, Joe's favourite flower. Austen was defeated in his chosen ward.

The progress of the trade unionist W.J. Davis from a member of the school board to a likely member of the cabinet is viewed here with dismay by Jesse Collings, whose Bordesley seat he would contest. In the event Davis failed in his attempt to unseat Collings.

The *Owl* humorously depicts an avaricious doctor touting for business.

After a local newspaper drew attention to the unlit and filthy courts in the city centre, the mayor Francis Clayton and a party of councillors made an evening visit with the result that gas lighting was installed.

Paradise Street. The Birmingham and Midland Institute, the town hall and Christ Church can be seen in turn.

A scene outside the Grand Theatre in Corporation Street. Andrew Melville, who owned the theatre, was described as 'the most popular man in the city.'

The Bull Ring on a market morning.

Looking down New Street

High Street (looking towards Dale End)

Colmore Row

The Theatre Royal, New Street, where pantomimes attracted full houses.

The assembly rooms in Edgbaston, a popular venue for balls and concerts.

The procession of the Shah of Persia through Small Heath, July 1889.

The departure of the Shah from New Street Station. The Shah is pictured slightly-to-the-right-of- centre; the mayor Richard Cadbury Barrow is on the left and behind him the town clerk Edward Orford Smith. The Shah was assassinated in 1896.

Francis Clayton, chairman of the finance committee and, in 1889-90, mayor.

Joseph Rowlands, 'a capital specimen of a man'; well-known in Birmingham as a solicitor and a Tory.

Index

About the Author

$\mathcal{S}$tephen Roberts is an Honorary Lecturer at the Research School of Humanities and the Arts in the Australian National University. He is the author of nine books and the editor of a further nine, amongst them *The Chartist Prisoners* (2008), *The Parliamentary Career of Charles de Laet Waldo Sibthorp 1826-1855* (2010) and *The Dignity of Chartism: Essays by Dorothy Thompson* (2015).

THE BIRMINGHAM BIOGRAPHIES SERIES

Already published:

Dr J.A. Langford 1823-1903: A Self-Taught Working Man and the Sale of American Degrees in Victorian Britain. 65 pp, 8 photographs, 2014. ISBN: 978 1495475122. £5.99.

Sir Benjamin Stone 1838-1914: Photographer, Traveller and Politician. 102 pp, 20 photographs, 2014. ISBN: 978 1499265521. £7.99.

Mocking Men of Power: Comic Art in Birmingham 1861-1914. 60 cartoons, 2014. ISBN: 978 1502764560. £8.99. (with Roger Ward)

Sir Richard Tangye 1833-1906: A Cornish Entrepreneur in Victorian Birmingham. 65 pp, 2015. ISBN: 978-1512207910. £4.99.

Joseph Chamberlain's Highbury: A Very Public Private House, 44pp, 2015. ISBN: 978-1515044680. £3.99.

Now Mr Editor!: Letters to the Newspapers of Nineteenth Century Birmingham. 100 pp, 2015, ISBN: 978-1518685897. £6.99.

Joseph Gillott: And Four Other Birmingham Manufacturers 1784-1892. 98 pp, 2016. ISBN: 1539483069. £6.99.

These books can be ordered from Amazon and other booksellers.

26382206R00050

Printed in Great Britain
by Amazon